Lives ot the Saints

Infant of Prague
with Prayers and Devotions

Edited by
Mark Etling

**Regina
Press**

Nihil Obstat: Reverend Robert O. Morrissey, J.C.D.
                 Censor librorum
                 May 14, 2004

Imprimatur: Most Reverend William Murphy
                 Bishop of Rockville Centre
                 June 7, 2004

THE REGINA PRESS
10 Hub Drive
Melville, New York 11747

Florentine Collection™, All rights reserved worldwide.
Imported exclusively by Malco.

Printed in U.S.A.

ISBN: 0-88271-758-8

Introduction

*T*wo of the fundamental tenets of the Christian faith are belief in the Incarnation and the immanence of God. While these two concepts are usually thought to be too difficult and profound for the average believer to grasp, they are actually relatively simple to understand.

The Incarnation refers to the belief that God, the Almighty and sovereign Lord of the universe, chose to come among us as a flesh and blood person, a fully human being. The divine Son of God, the second Person of the Trinity, became a man in the person of Jesus of Nazareth. Christians believe that God revealed himself fully and completely in human form: "The Word was made flesh, and dwelt among us."

The belief in God's immanence is based in part on the doctrine of the Incarnation. To affirm the immanence of God means to believe that God is not a silent, distant deity, uninterested in this world's events. Rather, God is ever near at hand. The immanent God cares deeply about the world and its people. God loves each person passionately, like a devoted spouse or parent, and cares deeply about what happens to us at every moment.

Devotion to the Infant Jesus is a reflection of the belief in the Incarnation and the immanence of God. Veneration of the Infant is an implicit acknowledgement of the Incarnation, an affirmation that Jesus is God in the flesh. It also implies an awareness that God, present in the Child Jesus, remains close to us, near to us at all times.

When believers pray to the Infant of Prague, they are affirming something about themselves as well. Each one of us is capable of incarnating the loving presence of God in the world. And we help ourselves and others experience the immanence of God whenever we are kind, merciful and compassionate.

Wherever there is love, forgiveness, mercy, and justice, God is there, close at hand, in the flesh.

The Story of the Infant of Prague

*D*evotion to the Infant Jesus has been a part of Christian piety since the earliest days of the Church. Some of the greatest saints of the early Church — Augustine, Jerome, Pope Leo the Great — are known to have venerated the Christ Child. In medieval times St. Francis of Assisi, deeply moved during his meditation that God became a child, set up the first Nativity scene so as to represent the divine mystery of the Incarnation. St. Anthony of Padua likewise marveled at the Infant Jesus, and was reported to have held the Christ Child in his arms.

The exact origins of the statue of the Infant Jesus are unknown, but historians point to a small sculpture of the Child with a bird in his right hand carved around the year 1340.

Devotion to the Child Jesus grew in Spain in the sixteenth century, due to the influence of St. Teresa of Avila. A number of statues of the Child carved in Spain, made of wax, ivory, and bronze and dressed in the aristocratic style of the times, found their way to Prague, then the capital city of Bohemia.

One of these statues made its way into Bohemia and was donated to a Carmelite convent located in the Mala Strana district of Prague. From there it was obtained by Dona Isabella Manrique of Spain. She in turn gave it as a gift to her daughter, Duchess Marie Manrique, on the occasion of her wedding in 1556 to Vratislav of Pernstyn, a Czech nobleman. In 1587, the statue was passed to Marie's beautiful daughter Princess Polyxena of Lobkovice, again as a wedding gift.

In 1628 Brother John Louis of the Assumption, prior of the Carmelites of Prague, communicated to the sisters his inspiration that they should venerate the Child Jesus in a special way. Soon thereafter Lady Polyxena, now a widow preparing to retire to the castle of Roudnice, presented the statue to the Carmelites at the Church of the Virgin Mary the Victorious. It was approximately eighteen inches high and had a wax body adorned with a long gown. The Christ Child held a globe in his left hand, while giving a blessing with his right.

As she presented the statue, Lady Polyxena is reported to have said to the sisters, "I give you what I prize most highly in this world; honor and respect the Child Jesus and you shall never be in want."

Brother John Louis ordered that the statue be placed on the altar of the novices' oratory. There the Carmelite sisters assembled every day to praise the Christ Child. From this time on, the statue became known as the Infant Jesus of Prague.

Later in that same year of 1628, Prague was invaded by the Saxons and Swedes as part of the religious conflict known as the Thirty Years War. The Carmelites were forced to flee the city, and devotion to the Holy Infant ceased. The convent was plundered, and the image of the Infant was thrown onto a trash heap behind the altar of the church.

It was not until 1638 that a young priest named Father Cyril returned to Prague and found the statue, its hands missing, still buried in the ruins of the church. He cleaned the statue and replaced it in the oratory for veneration.

Once while he was praying before the statue, Father Cyril reported hearing the Infant Jesus say, "Have pity on me and I will have pity on you. Give me my hands and I will give you peace. The more you honor me, the more I will bless you."

Father Cyril prayed to obtain the necessary funds to repair the statue. Soon the priest reported hearing the Infant Jesus speak to him a second time, with the message: "Place me near the entrance of the sacristy and you will receive aid." Fr. Cyril did this and a few days later, through the generosity of benefactors, the statue was repaired.

After this time, veneration to the Infant Jesus increased greatly. By 1654 a chapel was built to accommodate the many faithful who wished to venerate the statue. A solemn coronation and procession with the Infant, now adorned with a crown of gold encrusted with jewels, was celebrated by Archbishop Josef Corta on April 4, 1655. The anniversary of this coronation has been celebrated ever since on the feast of the Ascension.

Over the years, Prague was to endure more wars and civil unrest, but the church and the Infant Jesus chapel were left unharmed. In 1744, for example, Prussian troops surrounded the city, prompting authorities to hurry to the Carmelite convent. They asked the prior to carry the statue in solemn procession through the streets in order to free the city from the invaders. An honorable surrender was quickly negotiated, and a few months later the Prussians left Prague. The residents of the city flocked to the church to thank the Child Jesus for sparing them.

In 1776, the altar was rebuilt of marble, and two huge sculptures of the Blessed Virgin Mary and St. Joseph were placed to the left and right of the altar. The Infant Jesus was placed in a glass case standing on a pedestal engraved with crystals, and surrounded by twenty angels in gold.

By this time, copies of the Infant of Prague statue had been sculpted and distributed throughout Europe. Devotion to the Infant would eventually flourish in India, the Philippines, Australia, and the Latin American countries. The devotion has now spread to all parts of the world.

In 1993, the Church of the Virgin Mary the Victorious was returned to the Carmelite sisters by the Knights of Malta, who had controlled it since 1784. Today, thousands of pilgrims travel to Prague to venerate the Infant.

Prayers to the Infant of Prague

Prayer to the Infant of Prague

O merciful Infant Jesus. I know of your miraculous deeds for the sick. In view of the many blessings and cures granted through the veneration of your holy Infancy, particularly in the city of Prague, I exclaim with great assurance: O most loving Infant Jesus, you can cure me if it is your will. Extend your holy hand and by your power take away all pain and infirmity.

Prayer of Thanksgiving

*D*ivine Infant Jesus, I know you love me and would never leave me. I thank you for your close presence in my life.
Miraculous Infant, I believe in your promise of peace, blessings, and freedom from want. I place every need and care in your hands.
Lord Jesus, may I always trust in your generous mercy and love. I want to honor and praise you, now and forever. Amen.

Novena Prayer to the Infant of Prague

*D*earest Jesus, little Infant of Prague, how tenderly you love us! Your greatest joy is to dwell among us and to bestow your blessing upon us. Though I am not worthy that you should help me, I feel drawn to you by love because you are kind and merciful.

So many who turned to you with confidence have received blessings and had their petitions granted. Behold me as I come before you to lay open my heart to you with its prayers and hopes. I present to you especially this request, which I enclose in your loving Heart *(state your request):*

Rule over me, dear Infant Jesus, and do with me and mine according to your holy will, for I know that in your divine wisdom and love you will arrange everything for the best. Do not withdraw your hand from me, but protect and bless me forever.

I pray you, all-powerful and gracious Infant Jesus, for the sake of your sacred infancy, in the name of your blessed Mother Mary who cared for you with such tenderness, and by the greatest reverence with which St. Joseph carried you in his arms, help me in my needs. Make me truly happy with you, dearest Infant, in time and in eternity, and I shall thank you forever with all my heart. Amen.

Prayer to the Infant Jesus of Prague

O divine Child of Prague, and still the great omnipotent God, I implore you through thy most holy Mother's most powerful intercession and through the boundless mercy of your omnipotence as God, for a favorable answer to the intention I so earnestly ask for in this prayer. O divine Child of Prague, hear my prayer and grant my petition.

Pray one Our Father and one Hail Mary.

Prayer to the Infant Jesus of Prague

O Jesus, Prince of Peace and Sovereign of the Universe, you chose to humble yourself and come into the world, not as a powerful ruler, but as a helpless infant. Grant us the grace of humility and gentleness before you and our brothers and sisters. Grant, too, O Lord, that we may always strive to achieve the virtue and innocence of your own childhood. Instill in us a growing faith in you, O Lord, and the strength to resist temptation in a world that so widely rejects you. Look upon us with compassion and forgive us our sins. Fill our hearts with kindness and understanding, especially for children, the aged and those we dislike or who dislike us.

O Jesus, who so loved children that you admonished us, "Unless you become like little children, you will not enter the kingdom of heaven," grant us a childlike faith and purity of heart. Give us the grace not only to pray fervently, but to help spread your Gospel by deed as well as word. Amen.

Prayer to the Infant Jesus of Prague

O Infant of Prague, who said, "The more you honor me, the more I will bless you," give us the strength to bear the burdens of daily life in this sinful world. Give us a firm purpose of amendment and a resolve to lead a better life. Help us endure our afflictions and sorrows with patience and courage. Finally, O beloved Infant King, if it be your will, grant my petition *(state your request).* But whatever you choose, give me the strength to submit to your will in all things. Amen.

Prayer to the Miraculous Infant Jesus of Prague

*O*ur blessed Savior, Jesus Christ, instructed us, "Unless you turn and become like children, you will not enter the kingdom of heaven" (Matt. 18:3). Our divine Master not only taught us by word, but gave us his life as an example. He came among us as a helpless infant, the better to gain our affection and win our love. As a little child, he was still our God and already by right the Lord of the Universe he had created and now had come to recreate.

Devotion to our Savior, the Infant of Prague, honors the great mystery of his Incarnation. We acknowledge his divinity and his humanity, and rejoice in his great love that led him to give his life for us.

Prayer to the Infant Jesus of Prague

*L*ittle Infant Jesus of good health, God of love born to suffer for me!

In you above all do I find the courage and strength I need in the trials and troubles that weigh so heavily upon me.

By the sorrows of your most holy Mother, I implore you to lighten the burdens of my soul with your holy consolations and to relieve my bodily infirmities with your merciful kindness, if it so pleases the will of our Father in heaven. Amen.

Prayer to Father Cyril

*J*esus, unto thee I flee,
Through thy Mother praying thee
In my need to succor me.
Truly, I believe of thee
God thou art with strength to shield me;
Full of trust, I hope of thee
Thou thy grace wilt give to me.
All my heart I give to thee,
Therefore, do my sins repent me;
From them breaking, I beseech thee,
Jesus, from their bonds to free me.
Firm my purpose is to mend me;
Never more will I offend thee.
Wholly unto thee I give me,
Patiently to suffer for thee,
Thee to serve eternally.
And my neighbor like to me
I will love for love of thee.
Little Jesus, I beseech thee,
In my need to succor me,
That with Joseph and Mary
And the angels, I may thee
Once enjoy eternally. Amen.

Prayers Revealed by Our Lady to the Venerable Father Cyril

O Infant Jesus, I have recourse to you and ask you through the intercession of your holy Mother to help me in my need *(state your request)*, for I firmly believe that your divinity can help me.

I hope, in complete trust, to obtain your holy grace. I love you with all my heart and with all the strength of my soul. I am truly sorry for all my sins and beg you, O good Jesus, to give me strength to conquer them. I shall never offend you and I am ready to suffer rather than to cause you pain.

From now on I want to serve you with complete faithfulness and for love of you, O divine Child, I will love my neighbor as well as myself. Omnipotent Child, Lord Jesus, again I implore you, help me in this need of mine *(state your request)*.

Give me the grace of possessing you eternally with Mary and Joseph, and of adoring you with the holy angels in your heavenly court. Amen.

Effacious Prayer to the Holy Child Jesus

O Child Jesus, I have recourse to you through your holy Mother; I implore you to assist me in this necessity, for I firmly believe that your divinity can assist me. I confidently hope to obtain your holy grace. I love you with my whole heart and soul. I am heartily sorry for my sins, and ask you, O good Jesus, to give me strength to overcome them. I am firmly resolved never to offend you again and to suffer everything rather then displease you. Henceforth, I wish to serve you faithfully. For love of you, O divine Child, I will love my neighbor as myself. O Jesus, omnipotent Child, I beg you again to come to my assistance in this necessity *(state your request)*.

Grant me the grace of possessing you eternally with Mary and Joseph, and of adoring you with the holy angels and saints. Amen.

The Little Crown of the Infant Jesus of Prague

*V*enerable Sister Margaret of the Blessed Sacrament, a Carmelite sister who died in 1648, received a private revelation in which she was given a chaplet in honor of the Infant of Prague. This chaplet, known as the Little Crown, consists of fifteen beads. Three beads are in honor of the Holy Family. On these the Lord's Prayer is prayed. The other twelve beads are in honor of the holy childhood of Jesus, and the Holy Mary is prayed on each of them.

Before each of the Lord's Prayers, pray the words:

And the Word was made flesh.

Before the first of the Hail Marys, pray the words:

And the Word was made flesh
and dwelt among us.

On the medal, pray the words:

Divine Infant Jesus, I adore your cross, and I accept all the crosses you will send me. Adorable Trinity, I offer you for the glory of the Holy Name of God all the adorations of the Sacred Heart of the Holy Infant Jesus.

Consecration to the Holy Child of Prague

O divine Child Jesus, only-begotten Son of the Father, you are the true light that enlightens everyone coming into this world. It is through you that I am, it is through you that all things have been made, and without you nothing would be. It is therefore just that I devote myself to you without reserve.

In gratitude for all the love with which you love me, I devote to you all the love my heart is capable of. I ardently desire to love you still more, to offer you a heart more worthy of you. Accept this ardent desire, O amiable Child, and kindly bless it.

You have suffered for us and have borne our infirmities, in order that we might one day deserve to be associated with your eternal happiness. I want to unite my sufferings to yours, so that you may give them merit and they may be sanctified. As you have been weeping for me because of my sins, help me by your grace to weep for them myself.

I also devote to you all my joys. I only have the ambition and the will to seek those pleasing to your service, by the practice of the virtues taught in the mysteries of your divine childhood. I beg you to help me by your grace to acquire the gentleness, the humility, the childlike simplicity, the filial confidence and the perfect obedience, of which you give me such a splendid example.

May I progress in holiness and one day possess the rewards promised in heaven to those who practice the lessons of your holy childhood. Amen.

A Morning Offering to the Holy Child

O dear sweet Infant Jesus, I offer you my will, that you may strengthen it, my mind that you inspire it; my memory that you fill it; my wishes and desires, that you cleanse them; my intentions that you guide them, all my inner and outer activities, that you make them sacred. All I am and all I have is yours. Your love for me is my hope and trust. Hear me and grant that I may never leave you. Amen.

Novena to the Child Jesus

Day One

O sweet Child Jesus, here at your feet is a person who, conscious of my nothingness, turns to you, who are all. I have so much need of your help. Look on me, O Jesus, with love, since you are all-powerful. Help me in my poverty.

Our Father . . .
Hail Mary . . .
Glory Be . . .

By your divine infancy, O Jesus, grant the grace that I now ask *(state your request)* if it is according to your will and for my true good. Do not look upon my unworthiness, but rather on my faith, and show me your infinite mercy.

Day Two

O splendor of the heavenly Father, in whose face shines the light of the divinity, I adore you profoundly and I confess you as the true Son of the living God. I offer you, O Lord, the humble homage of all my being. Grant that I may never separate myself from you, my highest goal.

Our Father . . .
Hail Mary . . .
Glory Be . . .

By your divine infancy, O Jesus, grant the grace that I now ask *(state your request)* if it is according to your will and for my true good. Do not look upon my unworthiness, but rather on my faith, and show me your infinite mercy.

Day Three

O holy Child Jesus, in gazing upon your face, from which comes the most beautiful of smiles, I feel myself filled with a lively trust. I hope for all from your goodness. O Jesus, shed on me and on those dear to me your smile of grace and I will praise your infinite mercy.

Our Father . . .
Hail Mary . . .
Glory Be . . .

By your divine infancy, O Jesus, grant the grace that I now ask *(state your request)* if it is according to your will and for my true good. Do not look upon my unworthiness, but rather on my faith, and show me your infinite mercy.

Day Four

O Child Jesus, whose forehead was adorned with a crown of thorns, I accept you as my absolute sovereign. I do not wish to serve the evil one, my passions, or sin any longer. Reign, O Jesus, over this poor heart and make it all yours forever.

Our Father . . .
Hail Mary . . .
Glory Be . . .

By your divine infancy, O Jesus, grant the grace that I now ask *(state your request)* if it is according to your will and for my true good. Do not look upon my unworthiness, but rather on my faith, and show me your infinite mercy.

Day Five

I gaze upon you, O Redeemer, dressed in a mantle of purple. It is your royal attire. How it speaks to me of the blood you have shed for me and for all humanity. Grant, O Child Jesus, that I may respond to your great sacrifice and not refuse when you offer me some difficulty to suffer with you and for you.

Our Father . . .
Hail Mary . . .
Glory Be . . .

By your divine infancy, O Jesus, grant the grace that I now ask *(state your request)* if it is according to your will and for my true good. Do not look upon my unworthiness, but rather on my faith, and show me your infinite mercy.

Day Six

O most lovable Child, in contemplating you as you sustain the world, my heart fills with joy. Among the innumerable beings that you sustain, I also am one. You look upon me, uphold me at every instant and guard me as your own. Look after me, O Jesus, and help me in my many necessities.

Our Father . . .
Hail Mary . . .
Glory Be . . .

By your divine infancy, O Jesus, grant the grace that I now ask *(state your request)* if it is according to your will and for my true good. Do not look upon my unworthiness, but rather on my faith, and show me your infinite mercy.

Day Seven

*O*n your chest, O Child Jesus, shines a cross. It is the standard of our redemption. I also, O divine Savior, have my cross that, although light, very often weighs me down. Help me to bear it, and may the carrying of it be fruitful. You well know how weak and worthless I am.

Our Father . . .
Hail Mary . . .
Glory Be . . .

By your divine infancy, O Jesus, grant the grace that I now ask *(state your request)* if it is according to your will and for my true good. Do not look upon my unworthiness, but rather on my faith, and show me your infinite mercy.

Day Eight

*T*ogether with the cross, O Child Jesus, I see on your chest a little golden heart. It is the image of your heart, which is truly golden on account of its infinite tenderness. You are the true friend who generously gives himself for the one he loves. Continue to pour out on me, O Jesus, the enthusiasm which your love inspires, and teach me to respond always to your great love.

By your divine infancy, O Jesus, grant the grace that I now ask *(state your request)* if it is according to your will and for my true good. Do not look upon my unworthiness, but rather on my faith, and show me your infinite mercy.

Day Nine

*H*ow many blessings, O little Child, has your almighty right hand poured out on those who honor you and call upon you. Bless me also, O Child Jesus, in both body and soul. Bless and help me in my necessities, and grant me what I now desire. Listen with compassion to my prayers and I will bless your holy name every day.

Our Father . . .
Hail Mary . . .
Glory Be . . .

By your divine infancy, O Jesus, grant the grace that I now ask *(state your request)* if it is according to your will and for my true good. Do not look upon my unworthiness, but rather on my faith, and show me your infinite mercy.

Prayer to Be Prayed By a Sick Person

O most loving Infant Jesus, you can cure me if you will. Do not hesitate, O heavenly Physician, if it be your will that I recover from this present illness; extend your most holy hands, and by your power take away all my pain and infirmity, so that my recovery may be due to you alone.

If, however, in your mysterious wisdom you have determined otherwise, then at least restore my soul to health, fill me with heavenly consolation and blessing, that I may be like you, O Jesus, in my sufferings, and may your providence protect me until you, at the time of my death, bestow on me eternal life. Amen.

Prayer to Be Prayed By a Sick Person

O holy Child Jesus, lord of life and death, I bow before you, unworthy that I am, to implore you to cure *(name the person for whom you are asking this blessing)* who is so dear to my heart.

He (she) is in great suffering, wracked with pain, and can find no relief except in you, in whom he (she) places his (her) hope. Relieve him (her) in his (her) agony, O heavenly Doctor, free him (her) from his (her) suffering and give him (her) perfect health, if it be your will and for the good of his (her) soul. Amen.

Our Father . . .
Hail Mary . . .
Glory Be . . .

Prayer By a Sick Person for Healing

O most dear and sweet Infant Jesus, behold me, a poor suffering person who, sustained by a lively faith, invokes your divine aid to cure my infirmity. I put all my trust in you. I know that you can do all things and that you are most merciful, indeed you are yourself Infinite Mercy. O great little Infant, for the sake of your divine virtue and the immense love you bear for all the suffering, the oppressed and the needy, hear me, bless me, help me, console me. Amen.

Glory Be *(three times)*.

Prayer to the Infant of Prague

O miraculous Infant Jesus, prostrate before your sacred image, we ask you to cast a merciful look on our troubled hearts. Let your tender heart, so inclined to pity, be softened by our prayers, and grant us the grace for which we ardently implore you. Take from us all affliction and despair, all trials and misfortunes with which we are laden. For your sake hear our prayers and send us consolation and aid, that we may praise you with the Father and the Holy Spirit forever and ever. Amen.

A Prayer to the Child Jesus

O holy Infant Jesus, who shed your blessings on whoever invokes your name, look kindly on us who kneel humbly before your holy image, and hear our prayers. We commend to your mercy the many poor and needy people who trust in your divine heart.

Lay your all-powerful hand upon them and help them in their needs. Lay your hand upon the sick, to cure them and sanctify their suffering; upon those in distress, to console them; upon sinners, to draw them into the light of your divine grace; upon all those who, stricken with grief and suffering, turn trustingly to you for loving help.

Lay your hand also upon all of us and give us your blessing. O little King, grant the treasures of your divine mercy to all the world, and keep us now and always in the grace of your love.

Prayer for a Student

O Infant Jesus, eternal wisdom made flesh, who shed your blessings so generously on all, and most especially on school children and students who trust in you, please look kindly on me as I implore you to guide and assist me in my studies.

You, O God made man, Lord of all learning, source of all understanding and memory, come and help me in my weakness. Enlighten my mind, give me a ready ability to acquire knowledge and truth and the capacity to remember all I learn. Be my light, strength and comfort in moments of special difficulty.

By the grace of your divine Heart may I do all my school tasks to the best of my ability and gain the utmost profit from them, so that I may get good grades and advance in school. To merit such favors, for my part I promise to perform faithfully all my duties as a Christian and to love you more and more. O sweet Infant Jesus, keep me always under your protecting mantle and be my guide, not only on the path of learning, but above all on the path to eternal salvation. Amen.